Acknowledgements

To my parents, for inculcating values of resilience, patience, and unconditional support.

To my children, Pinaz and Piran for being constant sources of inspiration and love.

The publisher, without which this wouldn't have been possible.

I am grateful to the young models Sandeep Menon and Divya Menon, class 8th students of Arya Vidya Mandir, Bandra West Mumbai. They regularly participate in yoga sessions their school and possess good knowledge of yoga.

Sandeep Menon, a keen student, excelling in academics as well as in Art, Elocution, Dramatics and has won a national prize in Robotics.

Divya Menon, a keen swimmer and a trained Ballerina and has performed for Royal School of Ballet, London.

To my well wishers a word of appreciation.

Author

Asato Ma Sat Gamaya
Tamaso Ma Jyotir Gamaya
Mrityor Ma Amritam Gamaya
Om Shantih Shantih Shantih !

Meaning

O LORD! Lead me from the Unreal to Real
From Darkness to Light
From Mortality to Immortality
Om Peace Peace Peace !

YOGA for Children

Specially Designed
for School Co-corricular Activity
&
for Young Yoga Enthusiast

Rupa Chotrani
Yoga and Naturopath Consultant

ALLIED PUBLISHERS PVT. LTD.
New Delhi • Mumbai • Kolkata
Chennai • Bangalore • Hyderabad

ALLIED PUBLISHERS PRIVATE LIMITED

Regd. Off.: 1/13-14 Asaf Ali Road, **New Delhi**–110002
Ph.: 011-23239001 • E-mail: delhi.books@alliedpublishers.com

17 Chittaranjan Avenue, **Kolkata**–700072
Ph.: 033-22129618 • E-mail: cal.books@alliedpublishers.com

15 J.N. Heredia Marg, Ballard Estate, **Mumbai**–400001
Ph.: 022-42126969 • E-mail: mumbai.books@alliedpublishers.com

No. 25/10, Commander-in-Chief Road, Ethiraj Lane (Next to Post Office)
Egmore, **Chennai**–600008,
Ph.: 044-28223938 • E-mail: chennai.books@alliedpublishers.com

P.B. 9932, 1st Floor, Sunkada Chickkana Complex,
Loop Lane Off Race Course Road, Next to Hotel Maurya, Gandhi Nagar,
Bangalore - 560009
Ph.: 080-22262081 • E-Mail: bngl.books@alliedpublishers.com

Sri Jayalakshmi Nilayam, No. 3-4-510, 3rd Floor (Above More Super Market)
Barkatpura, Telangana, **Hyderabad**–500027
Ph.: 040-27551811, 040-27551812 • E-mail: hyd.books@alliedpublishers.com

Website: www.alliedpublishers.com

Revised Edition, 2020

ISBN: 978-81-8424-445-8

Published by Sunil Sachdev and printed by Ravi Sachdev at Allied Publishers Pvt. Ltd. 1/13-14 Asaf Ali Road, New Delhi - 110002

Preface

Dear Yoga Students,

They say,

> *Corporate whiz kids relax with it,*
> *Patients recoup with it,*
> *Weight watchers slim down with it,*
> *Warriors chill with it,*
> *Sages find GOD with it.*

Unlike what you think (and unlike what most people think) Yoga is not something boring, nor is it about going to Ashrams and doing *asanas*. No, in fact Yoga now has a lot of glamour attached to it. Celebrities like Julia Roberts, Meg Ryan, Richard Gere, Pierce Brosnan, and loads of supermodels, pop divas are all in to yoga. Even our late Prime Minister, Mrs. Indira Gandhi practiced yoga daily. This definitely helped her to get a cool mind to run the country.

Well, these are just a few names but they showcase the importance of this age old practice. They all use Yoga as a tool to cope up with their anxieties of stressful public life, to graduate them from distress to de-stress. To make them look good, feel good, help them improve relationships with everyone around them, and lastly but not the least, to increase their life span.

Actually, Yoga is all about self-development through mind and body control. Remember the movie "Matrix"? Allow me to tell you that the "Matrix" is a pretty ordinary thing compared to what Yoga can achieve. I know you may find it hard to this but wait until you read all about it.

Yoga is ancient but it is based on authentic scientific principles. It goes to the very heart of the greatest mystery of modern science—the mind-body interface—the original hardware of our body. The question is, is the human body like a computer the way some scientists tell us. Or, is there more to human beings than such a soulless scientific view? Well then, join me on this grand adventure and find out the answers yourself.

Are you interested? Then read on and have a real adventure.

> This book on Yoga may not replace personal coaching, but hopefully it will give you a basic understanding of the great enrichment of yoga studies and may be able to generate an abiding interest in you to make it a part of your life.

Contents

Science of Yoga

What is Yoga?

"The time has come", the Yogi said,
"To talk of many things,
Of Yama and Niyama,
Of postures and Pranayamic links,
Why the topsy-turvy pose,
And whether Yogis are fitness fiends?"

Yoga is an ancient Indian science. Historians have found a sculpture of a man sitting in meditation dating back to 2300 B.C. It is mentioned in the Rig Veda and Upanishads, which are considered to be the oldest and sacred texts in India. The evidence of its practice in Mohenjodaro and Harrappa indicates its antiquity.

Patanjali, a philosopher and a grammarian is considered the father of Yoga. He explained his Yogic philosophy in his famous book the "*Yoga Sutras*". Around the second century B.C. the general tenets of yoga may well have been fully formulated in ancient India. Patanjali is credited with gathering these and putting all of it together in the form of his now famous Yoga sutras.

To begin with, Yoga was only one of the six different systems of Indian philosophy. However, it soon acquired greater importance because of its usefulness in daily life and its relevance for even the common person. As we shall see, there are a number of stages in yoga and they are all useful in themselves. One does not have to reach the ultimate stage in yoga to derive the benefits of the early stages. This is also the reason for its newfound popularity in the West.

The Importance of Yoga

It is important to realize right at the outset that yoga is a complete way of life. It is not just a system of exercises or a physical culture regime. However, yoga benefits even the beginner, since it starts from the very basics. Yoga is not just about the body or physical excellence. Yoga deals with all the aspects of our being. Yoga not only develops the intellect but also the emotional and the creative side within us. Yes, this helps us to look at the brighter side of our lives all the times.

You must have seen athletes taking part in the Olympics. All these athletes are in peak physical condition when they participate at that level. However, this is never enough to bag a coveted Olympic medal. So what is it that sets the champions apart? Well, a part of the answer is the mental edge that true champions bring to their sport. Yoga is that magic discipline which can help all of us to acquire and keep that winning edge in life. Yes, success is achieved twice, once in the mind and second time in the real world.

I will give you another example, that of grandmaster Vishwanathan Anand. In his case, too every opponent of his is rated the best in the world. One requires immense concentration power. For this, he must be mentally very strong and focused but along with it, he has to be physically fit too for him to be able to concentrate. Any physical ailments would distract him and may result in his defeat. So, how does Yoga help? You would ask again. Before answering your question let me, first explain to you, the meaning of Yoga.

The Meaning of Yoga

Yoga originated from the Sanskrit word "yuj" that simply means "yoke" i.e. to join or unite. A yoke is a wooden framework, which joins two animals like oxen, at the neck for working together. Similarly, Yoga is an instrument to build healthy, strong and flexible bodies and minds.

Now, I will explain as to what role Yoga plays in making you a champion and gives you that winning edge. By practicing yoga, one not only develops one's physical fitness but trains the mind too. There is union of mind and body, and therefore no conflict is felt. It is due to yoga, that a mind and body interface is developed which helps us to conquer the world.

Sage Patanjali's Ashtanga Yoga

Patanjali, in his famous book *yoga sutra,* tells us about the eight fold *(astha)* path of Yoga.

1. Yama
2. Niyama
3. Asana
4. Pranayama
5. Pratyahara
6. Dharna
7. Dhyana
8. Samadhi

These eight stages are usually followed in a sequence and therefore called "*sutras*" which literally means a thread.

Benefits of these eight stages are enormous. You must have heard about it or seen it in the movies, the magical great Indian rope trick. However, did you know that it is highly possible due to the complete control over mind and body? This is gained by practicing these eight stages. It is unthinkable for a non-practitioner of yoga but for a Yogi it is achievable. As they say, Yoga impels you to do things you never thought you were capable of doing. It is all a mind game.

These eight stages are time consuming and your hectic schedule may not permit you to practice all the eight stages, but hey! the good news is that the first four sutras summarize the most useful aspect of this science in our modern day living.

Now, allow me to introduce these concepts to you in short.

1. Yama

These are called the universal moral commandments. It tells us about truthfulness, not causing injury to living things, avoidance of theft, keeping off temptations. It helps to develop an attitude of gratitude for what one has.

Yama includes the following:

- Ahimsa (non-violence)
- Satya (truth)
- Asteya (non-stealing)
- Brahmacharya (self-control)
- Aparigraha (non-greed).

2. Niyama

This is self-purification through discipline. Niyama tells us about purity both internal and external, contentment, keeping the mind calm, self-study and worshipping GOD everyday and not only during exams. In short, try to simplify your life and not be lured by attachments.

Niyama includes the following:

- Sauca (cleanliness)
- Santosh (contentment)
- Tapa (fortitude)
- Svadhyaya (self-study)
- Ishwarpranidana (surrender to the will of God).

Well, to get back where I had left, Yama and Niyama are the foundation of a well-balanced personality. Regular practice is needed, as they prepare us for the higher steps of Yoga.

3. Asanas

It is the practice of postures. Yoga is generally misunderstood as consisting only of *asanas*. The aim of Yoga is to systematically exercise each part of the body. It is considered as the vital instrument for balancing and harmonizing the basic structure of the human body.

As mentioned earlier, it consists of various physical postures which when performed, releases tensions, improves flexibility and maximizes the much-needed positive energy:

- Standing
- Sitting
- Lying down
- Inverted

- Twisting
- Back bending
- Balancing

Each of these gives us tremendous benefits. Some of these will be discussed in the later chapters.

4. Pranayma

It is the control and regulation of breathing. Here, one tries to control the most elementary functions of the subconscious mind—"breathing". We concentrate on our breathing while we concentrate on our mind. The side advantages are—greater concentration, and retention power, as these *asanas* purify the mind by removing the distractions. It provides a lot of oxygen to the brain cells thereby developing a strong mind. Which in turn helps us to stay focused on the task at hand and handle problems peacefully.

Following are a little advanced stages, the importance of which I have mentioned earlier.

5. Pratyahara

It occurs during meditation. It brings the senses under control from their respective outside destinations and helps to project those inwards. It's like your mind supervising the body.

According to Sage Patanjali, this is how our external senses come in close and direct contact with our mind. During this form of meditation, you win the battle with the distracting senses. After mastering pratyahara, you can practice dharna.

6. Dharna

It involves developing and extending the power of meditation. It is fixing of one's mind on an external object, which is possible only when you get rid of distractions, and your mind and senses are under control.

A well-known incident, which comes to my mind, is that of Guru Drona. Guru Drona was instructing his pupils, the young Kauravas and Pandavas princes, the science of archery. For a target, Guru Drona placed a wooden bird on the branch of a distant tree. He then asked his pupils to come forward one by one to test their skills and concentration.

First, he called Yudhishtra. "What do you see?" Drona asked, pointing to the target. Yudhishtra answered, "I see a blue sky, a tree, branches, leaves and a bird sitting amongst them." "Go back and sit down", snapped the Guru very annoyed. "There is no way that you will be able to hit the target." Then Guru Drona called the other princes one by one. "What do you see there?" he asked each one of them. Their replies were similar to Yudhishtra. "You are all unfit even to attempt to shoot this target", he said. Guru Drona then asked Arjuna. Arjuna looked at the target and said, "Guruji! I see only the right eye of the bird". Drona was pleased by his pupil's answer. "Good", he said, "now you must try and shoot the bird's eye." Arjuna concentrated his mind on the target, took a careful aim and managed to pierce the bird's eye with his first arrow.

Thus keeping the mind steady and concentrated, Arjuna was successful. Isn't this an important lesson to all of us?

7. Dhyana

Is the state of meditation, meditation on the object of concentration.

8. Samadhi

The ultimate stage of total absorption and therefore calmness. It is the state where the subconscious and conscious mind becomes one, and the resultant calmness leads to super consciousness. This is probably the state, which Gutama Buddha, achieved, the state of "Samadhi", sitting under a bodhisattva tree, like a flame in a windless spot.

Logic behind the Yogic Philosophy

Yogasana and Pranayama help purify the blood vessels by flushing out the toxins.

How does this happen?

While performing Yogic exercises, we turn and twist the body, stretch it tightly and release it. Through this process, our blood vessels get cleaned up. It helps the heart in pumping purified blood in to the body.

As we breathe in and out during Pranayama, the muscles of the lungs become elastic. This boosts their contracting and expanding power. They can absorb more oxygen. They burn up the toxins of the body and eject them in the form of carbon-di-oxide.

It is a known fact that Yogic exercises are probably the only system which aims to improve flexibility of spine.

You must have studied in your "biology lessons" that our spinal cord is the central axis of the body. It holds the key to all the nerve centers of the body. During Yogic asanas, which are generally carried out in slow and controlled motion, we tend to stretch and relax our physical structure fully. This frees the nerves from stress or strain and improves their functioning.

Bhavas

Yoga not only helps you achieve all the things that I have already told you, but much more as well, which you would find out soon.

Bhavas stand for a feeling or attitude. Bhava indicates an accompanying attitude towards a given technique, here the technique is in context of Yoga. These bhavas play a very important role on the path of yoga. Regular and repeated practice of these techniques of yoga slowly enhances the accompanying bhavas into one's personality.

Each one of us is born with positive and negative Bhavas. Let us talk about the positive bhavas.

1. *Dharma:* It is the duty which each one of us should recognize and follow.
2. *Jnana:* It is the path of knowledge.
3. *Vairagya:* It is detachment.
4. *Aishwarya:* It is achievement and satisfaction.

Here is a brief introduction of each of these four positive Bhavas and the associated asanas, which would help you achieve them.

1. Dharma

According to our oldest texts, the Vedas, Dharma means performance of 'duty' with a sense of responsibility.

The legend of Mahabharata throws light on this aspect of dharma. On the battlefield of Kurukshetra, Arjuna the great warrior and skilled archer, led the Pandava's army. Just as the battle was about to start, Arjuna hesitated at the sight of his relatives and teachers, now his sworn enemies. He broke down and refused to fight the battle, wanting to retreat (from responsibility). However, Lord Krishna, who was then acting as his Parathasarathy told him that as a warrior, it is his dharma to fight and as a king, he has certain responsibilities towards his fellowmen.

Therefore, Dharma is duty towards self, family and society.

All meditative asanas belong to this Bhava. (Padmasana, Sukhasana, Vajrasana).

2. Jnana

Jnana bhava, which develops through yoga, refers to yoga of the mind. It will arouse your curiosity, your awareness and therefore knowledge. You will find the process of enquiry to be fascinating and rewarding. It will also make you open minded and an intellectual. Yoga teaches our mind to self-analyze. Therefore, with a balanced state of mind of mental equipoise we arrive at solutions quickly.

Asanas involving upward and sideward stretches, asanas for the extremities of the body and pranayamas help us to achieve, Jnana Bhava. (Utakatasana, Talasana).

3. Vairagya

You must have heard this word in relation to saints, who renunciate the world and go to Kailash mountains for tapasya. However, in yogic context it means detachment.

How does a soldier perform his duty and how does he keep his conscience clear when he is in the battlefield? Every medical student is told in the beginning of his internship that he should not get emotionally attached to any patient as that will prevent him from taking right decision when required. The secret is detachment. You must have heard this famous verse from Rudyard Kipling's famous poem 'IF', it says: *If you can meet with triumph and disaster, and treat those two imposters just the same.* An attitude of detachment means the ability to remain calm and uninvolved on the emotional and mental levels. This does not mean that you are required to be indifferent and not care about anything. Instead, through yoga, you would have achieved even minded-ness, and therefore you are able to look at good or bad equally.

All the relaxation asanas, forward bending asanas, and asanas involving twisting of the spinal cord helps us achieve this Bhava. (Shavasana, Makarasana, Yoga-mudra).

4. Aishwarya

After achieving the first three Bhavas, viz dharma, jnana and vairagya, the feeling of achievement, satisfaction, and achieving knowledge and yet being humble refers to aishwarya bhava. All this adds great confindence to one's personality.

All asanas involving backward bending of the spine belong to this bhava. (Bhujangasana, Ushtrasana).

I know theoretically it is very difficult to understand but I am sure you would be able to experience these Bhavas through regular yogic practice.

Students, I will now take you to a Yogi who teaches *asanas* to people and guides them to perfection. You can call him Guruji as his pupils fondly call him. All the *asana* names are in Sanskrit and are derived from life and nature. Some *asanas* reflect the world of plants as in *vrkshasana* (the tree pose) or *padmasana* (the lotus pose). Other *asanas* bring out the movements of various animals, like *ushtrasana* (the camel pose), *marjariasana* (the cat pose), *simhagarjanasana* (the lion roar pose), to name a few.

Here comes Guruji. Namaste Guruji, I told you about my yoga students, who are very keen to learn a few *asanas*, which would help ease the every day stresses and apprehension of growing up; increase concentration, memory and stamina.

Guruji: Students, I am glad you came here. I feel children are natural yogis as they have greater flexibility and a great desire to learn new things. As you are growing up, your internal organs are also growing and can get upset due to diet changes and over stimulation of nerves due to changes in hormonal levels. Yoga helps keep all organs healthy despite daily stresses. As you know Yoga is unification of mind and body and with practice, it increases awareness. It helps to look within ourselves. It helps to trust yourself thereby you become more confident during a period of rapid change within you and are able to look at the world and participate with a positive outlook.

You seem very curious to know about the various kinds of *asanas* my pupils are performing here in this room.

Yoga Student: Yes, Guruji I am very keen. These asanas' poses remind me of the movements of various animals.

Guruji, do they bring about their attributes and energies of their animal equivalents?

Guruji: I would say in case of martial arts it does bring about the attributes and the energies but in case of Yoga, it brings out the agility due to the flexible spine one achieves.

Come, now I will take you around and introduce you to these fantastic *asanas,* which impart immense benefits.

Yoga Student: Guruji tell me about this topsy-turvy pose.

Guruji: This topsy-turvy pose is called *shirshasana*. This is a favourite *asana* of the yogis and is spectacularly beneficial in its effects. It is said that the practice of this asana brings one nearer to the spiritual consciousness. It tones up all the systems of the body particularly the nervous system.

Yoga Student: Definitely, this must be a very important *asana* as the nervous system governs the mental as well as the physical conditions of an individual.

Guruji: You are right, *Shirshasana* accelerates the circulation of blood and is a very important asana for memory besides imparting various other benefits.

Yoga Student: No wonder, my grandfather has such a sharp memory. He practices this asana regularly.

Guruji: Yes, there is no harm in doing this asana even up to 65 years of age once it has been mastered.

The next asana you see is *bhujangasana*. As the name suggests it resembles an irritated cobra. This asana curves the spine backwards thereby increasing its flexibility. To maintain the activity of youth even at an advanced stage, the spine should be kept supple and elastic. Flexibility of the spine is very important because, according to yogic philosophy a healthy spine creates balance and acts as a cradle for a healthy mind. When you practice various *asanas,* the spine practically moves in all the directions creating space, between the vertebral discs of your spine allowing a free flow of energy to various organs.

Yoga Student: Guruji, is Prabhu performing a locust pose?

Guruji: Yes, you are right. It is called *shalabhasana,* the locust pose. This is a unique pose where all the extensor muscles of the body get contracted while the flexor muscles get stretched and relaxed during the practice of this asana. In this pose, the abdomen supports the weight of the body and therefore bulging of the belly is prevented.

This *asana* arches the lower spine (lumbar) backwards and therefore helps to increase the flexibility of spine.

The next asana I will tell you about is *dhanurasana* also called the bow-pose. It is a combination of *shalabhasana* and *bhujangasana*. The complete pose presents the appearance of a bow with stretched wings. It is an excellent asana for the back and abdominal muscles. There are various other body parts, which also benefit and these are the thorax, lungs, thighs, knees, the list is endless.

The fourth *asana,* which you see Zaheed, performing is the *halasana* (hal-plough). The completed pose resembles a plough. The extended arms are like the blades of a ploughing machine, meant for making furrows in the ground. In addition, the extended legs beyond the head due to great arching of the trunk-form the propelling handles.

Yoga Student: I am sure this *asana* too makes the spine very flexible like others.

Guruji: Yes, it does make the spine supple and elastic and it also exercises all the muscles of the body. It helps to increase the secretions of all the glands in the abdomen and therefore is an invaluable asana to correct any stomach problems.

Yoga Student: Guruji, the asana being performed looks exactly like *halasana* to me.

Guruji: Yes, it does look like *halasana,* but only in the first stage. This asana is called *sarvagasana* (the shoulder stand pose). This asana is referred to as an all-body pose, as *sarvagasana* means complete body asana. Like others, this asana too has invaluable benefits like reducing varicose veins of legs, to regularize defective basal metabolism, reduce abdominal fat, and toning the muscles of the heart at the same time.

The next *asana* is generally practiced after *sarvangasana* and is called *matsyasana.* This *asana* is complementary to the previous *asana (sarvangasana).* The cleansing and reviving of the parts that are left unexercised by the previous *asana* are achieved by the practice of this pose. This *asana* provides a richer supply of oxygenated blood to the face and the brain. The enhanced oxygenated blood increases the secretions of the two endocrine glands, the *pituitary* and the *pineal.* Incidentally, the pose also develops the muscles of the back, waist and the neck.

My pupil Kavita, is practicing the *asana paschimottanasana.* This *asana* stretches all the posterior muscles of the body, particulary the muscles of the back and of the posterior wall of the abdomen. It has an excellent benefit for toning up sluggish bowels and abolishing constipation.

Asanas also increase the metabolic activity of the body by increasing the secretions of the endocrinal glands and are thus helpful in reducing fat. *Asanas* are also a good recuperative measure after any long illness; the *asanas* will brace up the body quicker than any other form of physical exercise.

I will now tell you a little bit about *yog-mudra asana.* It is highly praised by yogic literature. This is the best exercise to relieve constipation due to sluggishness of the large intestines. The position of hands and head in this peculiar pose, which consists of bending the body forwards, at the hip joint so as to touch the forhead to the ground, exerts pressure at the very points which are responsible for constipation. Daily practice of this pose in isolation at a particular hour, specially early in the morning will create a desire to open the bowels. Take care to evacuate the bladder first.

Yoga Student: Well Guruji, no doubt yogic asanas assure us of our physical well-being. It also provides us with several theraptic remedies to correct chronic constipation that occurs generally due to our hectic life style in which we tend to gobble down a burger instead of a meal.

Guruji: Occasionally it is all right, but when it becomes a part of your daily routine then the problem starts. During the growing up years, yoga is very useful as it eases out the tensions caused by stress of tight muscles, tendons and ligaments. The stress causes energy blocks, which causes headaches, irritability or even digestive upsets. These are eased away. Here I would like to mention a proven fact that yoga helps keep people more in tune with their bodies and eating habits and therefore those who practice yoga tend to avoid junk food and over-eating because they want to respect their bodies...

Yoga Student: Guruji, it is as if you are unfurling the most valuable facts from the Pandora's Box or shall I say Yogi's box. With all this information at hand, I already feel as if I have a solution to every problem in this world.

Guruji: Lastly, I will tell you something about *padmasan,* which is the foundation of all the meditation *asanas.* This *asana* is praised highly in yogic literature for its high spiritual value. In this pose, the physical benefits are restricted to only the lower extremities. In performing the foot-lock pose to resemble the petals of a lotus (hence the name, *padma*–lotus) one has to arrange the feet in a particular way and in doing so the knee joints and leg muscles are greatly exercised and massaged.

I can go on, as there are about eighty-four *asanas* in yogic literature of India. Though I hope, I have aroused enough interest in you and I sincerely hope it spurs you on to daily practicing these asanas. However, for your age group I have selected a set of few *asanas,* which will cover all the aspects of growing up and benefit you immensely.

Chakra Maze

(A journey through our energy centers)

Dear yoga students,

In yoga, neither body nor the mind is looked at in isolation. Today let us make a journey through our energy centers and get charged.

In Yoga, the focus is on energy—when energy is in harmony then both, the physical and mental state of our body will be in perfect health. Our body is like a battery, which does not need an external recharger but has a special built in device to recharge. It recharges through the energy centers called *chakras* by our yogis. *Chakra* is the Sanskrit word for wheel: These *chakras* are like spirals of energy. Each spiral is linked with each other, like the spirals of a spring. By yogic exercises, the hidden energy lying at the base of the spiral moves upwards, and the power of these *chakras,* increased manifolds. Scientifically these *chakras* are a part of our endocrine system. You must have read about it in your science textbooks. I will tell you briefly about the endocrinal system. All the organs in the endocrine system are glands. They are unique from other glands, because they release chemicals known as hormones into general circulation. There are seven endocrinal glands, they are: pineal glands, pituitary glands, thyroid glands, the thymus glands, the pancreas, the gonads, and the adrenal glands. The glands of the endocrine system are located in widely separated parts of the body. The hormones they release are important to body functions. The secretions from these seven magical glands (endocrine glands) in our body get mixed up with the blood to make us feel balanced and charged. You would be quite surprised to know these *chakras* or the secretions from these glands also mould our minds and character. A simple example is of the adrenalin glands when not functioning properly, tends to make us anxious or fearful of situations we face in our lives.

After this brief introduction, let us start with our journey. The seven *chakras* are eager to tell you more about themselves.

The *1st chakra (sahasrara)* introduces itself as the *crown chakra.* I am located at the top of the head also called the *pineal gland.* I am associated with the entire nervous system. I bring a sense of generosity in you.

The *2nd chakra (ajna)* the *brow chakra* says, I am placed in the center of the forehead and called the *pituitary gland.* I am related to the eyes and lower head and that is why I am also known as the *primitive 3rd eye.* I am your seat of true motivations.

The *3rd chakra* the *throat chakra (vishudhi)* says, I am located in the neck. Doctors call me the *thyroid gland.* I control the throat and the neck, the arms and the hands. I govern the intuitive growth in you.

Beating rhythmically the *4th chakra (anahata)* the *heart chakra* says, I am overlying your heart and called the *thymus gland.* I am believed to form a hormone to give you immunity. I arouse compassion and generosity in you.

The *5th chakra (manipura)* the *solar plexus chakra* says, I control all the organs below the diaphragm. I am scientifically known as *pancreas.* I lie behind the lower part of your stomach. I regulate the digestion of sugar by producing 'insulin'. The positive aspect of my functioning properly is that you gain confidence; you become an optimist and become alert.

The *6th sacral chakra (swadhisthana)* growled from the center of the belly. The endocrine gland I am associated is the *gonads,* I look after your reproductive system. I bring out sociable, joyful and independent character in you.

The *7th* and the last chakra, the *root chakra (muladhara)* says from the base of the spine. I am also called the *adrenal glands.* I relate to the *kidneys,* and the *bladder.* These are the endocrinal glands. These develop qualities like assertiveness, willpower and courage. Most important I control your stress levels.

This was the end of the journey through these amazing chakras and mind you, we can avail all the benefits by keeping them fit-n-fine with Yoga.

Be a Sport

Few people are aware of the real importance of playing games, and their impact on our lives. Games encourage imagination, social interaction and self-expression. They play a vital role in the development of a person's personality.

It is interesting to know that there is a relation between yoga and sports. A large number of professional sportsmen are now incorporating yoga in their training and practicing sessions. This not only enhances their self-confidence in their skills but also is useful for maintaining physical and mental health. *Asanas* by their very nature, affect major and minor muscle groups and organs as by giving you strength, increasing flexibility and bringing nourishment to internal organs. Although most poses are not aerobic in nature, they do in fact send orygen to the cells in the body by way of conscious deep breathing and sustained stretching and contraction of different muscle groups through various asanas.

Did you know that if your body is flexible and supple you will be less prone to sports injuries: Yes, that is because your joints will be kept lubricated, Let us take the example of tennis, a rachet sport. This sport often involves intense physical effort. Yoga would help you to relax and replenish your energies after a strenuous game of tennis. It also promotes calm, clear thinking, especially in situations that call for fast reactions. So, read on the ten benefits, practising yoga can do to a sports person.

1. Gives You Flexibility

Did you know, that increasing your flexibility with yoga leads to ease of movement and fewer injuries? It enables you to move freely with an improved range of motion.

2. Improves Your Balance

Most of the sports require pace and/or concentration, so that your body is able to move in any direction with ease within a split second. But if your body is off balance and the upper half of the body does not coordinate with the lower half, your response time increases. Many yogic postures like Tadasana, Parvatasana help you find your balance. These asanas strengthen your muscles, release physical tension and improve your concentration and poise. Yoga makes your limbs balanced, strong and relaxed.

3. Keeps You Focused

Yoga teaches the discipline of being present in the moment through the physical postures and breathing techniques. In learning to hold postures, you automatically become clearer in your mind. You learn to focus on what is happening that moment to your body, breath and mind. This skill of learning to be to the moment will help improve your game by allowing you to stay focused on the task. The famous world record holder of pole vault Sergei Bubka says, "I practice my breathing and focusing before every competition, which helps me to be present in the moment 100 per cent, during my turn in the event, this helps me achieve new heights of my capabilities."

4. Strengthens Your Body

Yoga requires your entire body to be working as one unit so that the strengthening of all the minor and major muscles groups takes place simultaneously. You'll find it much easier to move quickly and effortlessly in sports when your whole body feels strong as a unit.

5. Improves Your Mind/Body Connection

You already know that "yoga" means to yoke. In yoga you learn to control your body through your mind. The breath is an essential tool, which unites our body and mind. With this power packed tool, you can draw your mind and body back into union.

6. Helps Reduce the Stress

One of the quickest and most significant benefits of yoga is the effect it has on reducing stress. How does this affect your sports performance? When you are stressed, the body parts holds onto that stress, which you tend to feel in the neck muscles, back, hamstrings, stomach, head; well, just about anywhere. These tense muscles decrease the flexibility of our body. This in turn increases pain and risk of injury while playing. Yoga helps release stress in your body and mind so the body gets more freedom to perform at its best.

7. Gives You a Perfect Posture

As mentioned earlier, yoga is the only exercise, which strengthens your spine. Unlike a typical fitness routine, practically every posture in yoga has a positive effect on the spine. The stronger and more flexible your spine is, your posture automatically falls into proper alignment and thus your posture improves. This has a positive effect on every aspect of how you move, especially in sports where your quickness matters most.

8. Improves Your Perception

Through yoga, you become aware of your body and its movements. It definitely guides you in your game because it also helps you be more aware of both your teammates and your opponents.

9. Makes You Agile

Yogasana assists in improving your agility. The yogic exercises give your, body strength, flexibility, posture, balance and give your thinking process a clear perception, which in turn improves your body's agility.

10. Makes You a True Sportsman

Besides the physical and mental aspects of yoga, there is also a spiritual element. Yoga teaches you to connect with yourself and all living things around you. It teaches you comradeship, non-violence. Therefore, no matter whether you win or lose, you would live with a sense of appreciation for your competitors and a feeling of peace.

General Instructions

Some Do's and Dont's of Asanas

Before starting any *asanas,* consult a trained professional in Yoga if you have any medical problem.

1. Best time to do *asanas* is early in the morning half an hour after getting up—Yes! Your body needs some time to gear up after that long snooze. Or early evening also would do i.e., before dinner but not before your bed as Yoga would have a stimulating effect which may prevent you from sleeping.
2. Never exercise on a full stomach. That is because your digestive organs are putting in a lot of hard work in chomping the food you have eaten and secreting juices to digest them and sucking out all the nutrients to provide your body with that incredible energy. Therefore, you must wait at least for three hours after a main meal and one hour after eating a light snack.
3. The room in which you do your *asanas* should be well lit and well ventilated.
4. A mat is required as the floor would be too hard. Don't try the bed as it would be too soft.
5. Wear comfortable clothing as too tight clothing would restrict your flexibility as well as circulation to some areas of the body.
6. After finishing *asanas,* wait for quarter of an hour before eating, even if you get that whiff of lip smacking pizza which mummy has kept in the oven.
7. Avoid hot water bath immediately after Yoga, while a shower, which is just warm, is all right.

Basic Techniques

1. Do *asanas* slowly with no stress.
2. Breathe through your nose, unless otherwise told to do so.
3. Breathe slowly and deeply from your abdomen. When inhaling push out and while exhaling let it return.
4. Be aware and concentrate on your posture.
5. Be regular. Aim to do the routine six times a week.

Ready Steady and Go

Keep in Mind

Any project is taken up with a lot of enthusiasm, but in the first few days, you do not feel all that good and may feel slight aches and pains and a little stiffness here and there, but that's only because yogic exercises are causing the body to eliminate toxins. Remeber any discomfort will only be temporary.

So, do not dwindle and never give up.

Following are the set of asanas in standing poses, seated poses, lying down poses and some techniques for concentration.

Standing Asanas

Talasana

(Palm tree pose)

Guruji: 'Talasana', 'tada' means a palm tree. Therefore, it is also called, *Tadasana*. In this, the body pose resembles a palm tree. In addition, it is an important asana because from this *asana* all other standing poses begin and to which they return. Now follow these steps.

1. Stand erect with your feet one foot apart.
2. Keep your back straight and gently draw in your abdomen.
3. Stand on your toes and inhale slowly for the count of three. As you inhale stretch both your hands upwards above your head with palms facing each other and elbows straight.

4. Remain in this posture and count six while holding your breath.
5. Then while exhaling for three counts bring your hands and feet down simultaneously.
6. Repeat three times.

Benefit

Helps in increasing your height up to a certain age.

HASTAPADASANA
(Hand toe pose)

1. Stand with your feet together and at the count of three, while inhaling deeply, raise your arms above your head.
2. Without bending your knees, slightly move your hands backwards.
3. Exhale as you bend forward and hold your toes. Keep your head between your arms.
4. Hold this position and count until six.
5. Slowly inhale for the count of three and return to the starting position.

Initially you may not be able to reach your toes but with practice and increasing flexibility of your spine, nothing would be impossible.

Benefit

Helps to keep the spine supple.

Utkat Asana
(Chair pose)

Guruji: In this *asana* we pretend to be sitting in a chair and therefore it is called the "chair pose". Let us learn the pose.

1. Stand in *Tadasana.*
2. Keep your hands forward, elbows straight and palms facing downwards. While inhaling for the count of three stand on your toes.
3. Exhale and bend your knees, squatting down until your thighs are parallel with the floor (as if sitting on a chair).
4. Retain this pose for the count of six. Focus on stability.

5. While inhaling, slowly rise on your toes. Then bring your hands down and heels back on the floor.
6. Repeat three times.

Benefits

1. It helps in improving balance of our body, which indirectly keeps our mind calm and focused.
2. It strengthens the leg muscles thereby helping weak knees.
3. It creates awareness of breath and movement, which helps in concentration.

AKARNA DHANURASANA
(Bow and arrow pose)

Guruji: In this asana the body is stretched as if a string of an archery bow. This is how it is done:

1. Stand erect with the feet 6–12 inches apart and the arms at the sides.
2. Take a short step forward with the right leg.
3. Clench the right fist and raise the arm in front of the body, so that it is over the right foot and slightly above the eye level.
4. Clench the left fist and bring it slightly behind the right fist.
5. Gaze over the right fist as though holding a bow and arrow, and fix the eyes on an imaginary target.
6. Inhale and slowly pull the left fist back to the left ear, tensing both arms as if drawing the bow. Keep the

left elbow at shoulder level. Exhale and release the imaginary arrow.

7. Relax the neck and bring the left fist forward to the right fist.
8. Inhale while pulling back the bowsting and exhale while releasing the bowsting.

Benefits

1. It will exercise your shoulders, muscles of the neck and shoulder blades.
2. It strengthens the leg muscles.

EKAPADASANA

(One legged pose)

Guruji: Now I will teach you *ekpadasana* which means one (ek) legged (pada) pose (asana). It is also called the "tree pose". This is one of the poses, which helps us to develop balance in our bodies, which in turn is important to maintain the balance of different *chakras* or endocrinal glands as you would like to call them. At the time of growth, the body's chemistry is changing, the chakras are developing, and becoming more active, by releasing secretions called hormones. An imbalance in the secretions of these hormones leads to mood swings or may show up as a rebellious character.

The steps are:

1. Stand erect with feet together. Gaze at a point in front of you.
2. Lift your one leg; bend it at the knees. Rest the foot on the inner thigh of the other leg. Hold the standing knee strong and do not push the knee back.
3. Join your hands in front of your chest as if you do while praying, with elbows relaxed.
4. Breathe normally and remain in this posture as long as possible.
5. Change legs and repeat the asana.

Tips

In the beginning, you can always stand against the wall and take its support.

Benefits

1. It strengthens the leg and feet muscles.
2. It develops balance.

STHITAPRARTHANA—ASANA
(Steady pose)

Guruji: This pose means, to be steady as a mountain. This is the simplest of them and last of the standing *asanas.*

1. Stand straight with your feet together. Join your hands in front of your chest.
2. Relax your elbows and close your eyes.

3. Remain in this posture for two minutes and try to observe your breath.

Benefits

1. It will give similar benefits as in meditation.
2. It will bring steadiness to the body.
3. It will give you clarity of thoughts and therefore a feeling of self direction.

Sitting Asanas

Padmasana
(Lotus pose)

Guruji: This is an important meditative pose as mentioned earlier.

1. Sit on the ground with your legs stretched in front of you.
2. Lift the foot of right leg and place it on the thigh of the left leg.
3. Then lift the foot of the left leg and place it on the thigh of the right leg.
4. Gently close your eyes, relax your shoulders with your back straight.
5. Place your right hand on left hand and your hands placed near the abdomen and rest your hands on your feet.
6. Sit in this posture for three minutes and take your awareness on your breath.

Benefits

1. It will help you to strengthen the knee and ankle joints. It will help to correct tightness or weakness in these joints.
2. It develops an alertness of the mind.

Vajrasana
(Thunderbolt pose)

Guruji: Like the previous asana, this one is also a meditative pose. This asana is also very good for the legs as it removes the impurities accumulated in our shins and knees. It has a good effect on our digestive system.

1. Kneel down, keeping your back straight and shoulders relaxed.
2. Keep your knees together, heels apart, and toes touching each other. Place your hands on your knees.

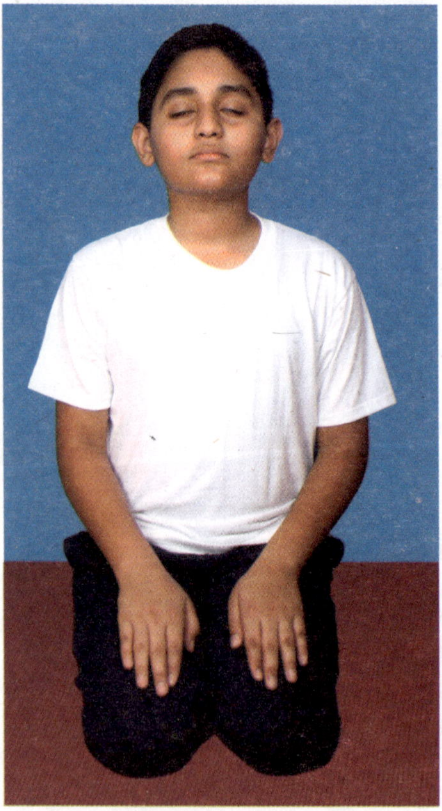

3. Sit on your heels.
4. Close your eyes and observe your breath.

Benefits

1. It helps to calm our mind.
2. It helps in keeping the spine upright.

Parvatasana
(Mountain pose)

Guruji: This asana is called the mountain pose as the name suggests.

1. Sit in any meditative pose, as per convenience. (*Padmasana, Sukhasana, Vajrasana*)
2. Keep your head straight, hands stretched at the side, palms facing downwards.
3. Breathe in deeply for three seconds. Stretch your arms up with your elbows straight.
4. Join your hands above your head and let your arms touch your ears.
5. Remain in this position for six seconds.
6. While exhaling for the count of three bring your arms back to your sides. Do not bend your elbows and keep your palms facing downwards.
7. Repeat three times.

Benefit

It helps to make the spine firm and strong.

Yoga Mudra
(Forward bending)

Guruji: This *asana* is simple but a fantastic exercise for all your stomach problems. It enhances the functioning of stomach, liver, and spleen. This is how you do it:

1. Sit in *sukhasana/padmasana.*
2. Hold the wrist of your left hand with your right hand at the back.
3. Inhale and expand your chest.
4. Exhale for three counts, twist your body to your right, bend and touch your forehead to your right knee. Relax your shoulders and stay in this position for the count of six.
5. Inhale slowly and come up to the count of three.
6. Repeat on the left side.
7. Inhale and come up.
8. Exhale, bend forward and touch your forehead to the floor.

9. Hold this position and count six.
10. Inhale and come up.
11. Repeat three times.

Benefits

1. It will make your digestive organs healthy.
2. The waist muscles are strengthened.
3. Develops humility.

Titali Asana
(Butterfly movement)

1. Sit in the base position.
2. Bend the knees and bring the soles of the feet together.
3. Keep the heels as close to the body as possible.
4. Place the hands on the knees.
5. Using the palms, gently push the knees down towards the floor, allowing them to spring up again.
6. Do not force this movement.
7. Repeat 20–30 times.
8. Breathe normally throughout the process.

Benefits

1. It prepares the legs for mastery of various other meditative *asanas*.
2. The inner thigh muscle tension is relieved.

Ushtra Asana
(Camel pose)

Guruji: *Ushtra* is a Sanskrit word, which means a camel; therefore, also called the camel pose.

1. Sit in *vajrasana*. Then, kneel down with your toes pointed outwards.
2. Inhale deeply for two seconds. Bend behind a little. Drop your hands one by one on the soles of your feet.
3. Hold for four seconds.
4. Exhale for two counts, bringing back one hand at a time.
5. Repeat three times.

Benefits

1. It is an excellent asana for relieving the tension from our neck muscles and strengthens them.
2. It also removes the stiffness in the shoulders.

MARJARI ASANA
(Cat pose)

1. As the name suggests get into a cat pose i.e., kneel down and then, rest your palms on the floor, fingers facing forward.
2. Inhale and count two, raise your head up and depress the spine.
3. Hold till four counts.

4. Exhale and count two, lower your head and stretch the spine upwards.
5. Repeat three times.

Benefits

1. Flexibility of the spine improves.
2. Reduces back pain.

Paschimottan Asana
(Back stretch pose)

Paschim = back, Tan = stretch

1. Sit on the floor, stretch your legs forward and rest your hands on your thighs.
2. Inhale for two seconds; raise your arms above your head. Let your arms touch your ears.
3. Exhale for two seconds; bend forward and touch your toes, keeping your knees straight.
4. Hold your breath for four seconds in this posture.
5. Inhale for two seconds and come up.
6. Repeat three times.

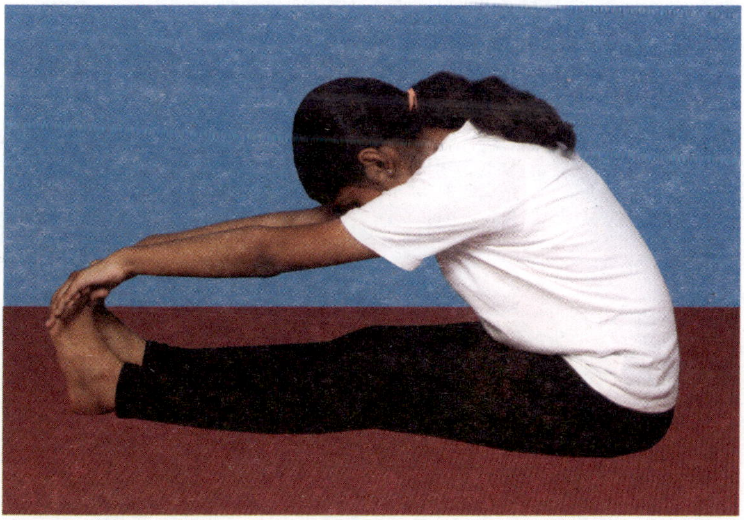

Tips

Take care not to overstrain the muscles. The gradual arching of the back more and more every day will make the necessary adjustments towards a perfect pose.

Benefits

1. Strengthens the knee joint muscles.
2. It massages the abdominal organs.

Gomukh Asana
(Cow face pose)

1. Sit on the floor. Fold your left leg in. Then fold your right leg over the left so that one knee is above the other.
2. Take your left arm over your head and bend it at the elbow. Place the left hand between your shoulder blades.
3. Then take your right hand behind your back. Clasp the fingers of your right hand with the fingers of your left hand.
4. Look straight and breathe normally.
5. Then change your hand and leg position.

Benefits

1. It relieves stiffness in the shoulders, neck and back.
2. It helps in improving the posture.
3. It alleviates cramp in the legs.

Simha Garjanasana

(Lion roar pose)

Guruji: I know you like singing, this asana, which I will show, will help you in developing strong and melodious voice.

Yoga Students: Melodious voice? Well, that would be great. However, Guruji the name of the *asana* suggests it has something to do with roaring.

Guruji: That is right, but the roaring will only exercise your vocal chords.

1. Sit in *Vajrasana* with your hands on the floor in front of your knees and palms downward.
2. Look in front, open your mouth wide and stretch your tongue out.
3. Then do the garjana (roaring) sound, just like a lion.
4. Slowly take your tongue inside and close your mouth.
5. Repeat two times.

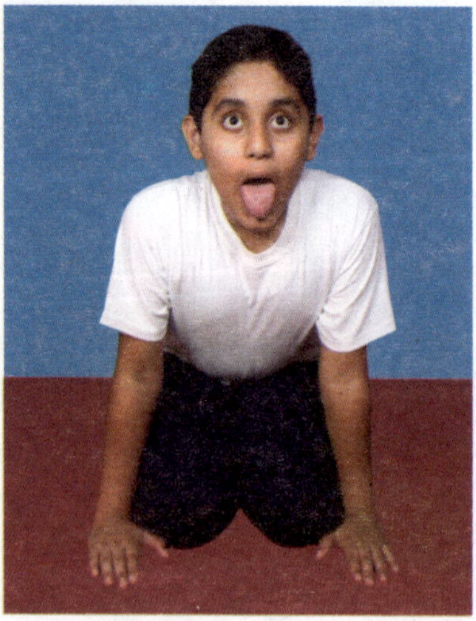

Benefits

1. It relieves problems of throat, even tonsils, nose, ear, eyes and mouth.
2. It helps in alleviating the problem of nervousness and that of stammering.
3. It helps in developing a strong and melodious voice.

Nauka-Sanchalan Asana
(Rowing the boat)

1. Sit on the floor with your legs stretched and your hands in fist position.
2. Inhale for two seconds and bend behind.
3. Exhale and make movements as if rowing a boat, bringing your arms down towards your feet.
4. Row forwards five times and in a reverse manner for five times.

Benefit

Exercises the abdomen thoroughly and massages the abdominal organs.

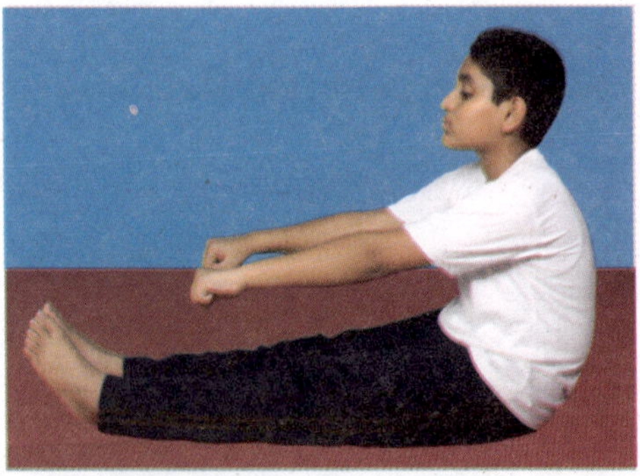

Lying Down Asanas

Padasanchalan Asana
(Cycle paddling)

1. Lie down flat on the floor.
2. Place your hands by your side.
3. Raise both the legs. Bend the knees and do the cycling movements as though peddling a bicycle.
4. Repeat the movements 10 times in a forward direction and 10 times in reverse direction.
5. Breathe normally throughout.

Benefits

1. Helps in strengthening the knee joints.
2. Strengthens the abdominal muscles.

Matyasana
(Fish pose)

1. Lie flat on the floor with your legs crossed i.e. in *sukhasana/padmasana.*
2. Slowly lift yourself, arch your back, rest the elbows on the floor and touch the crown of the head to the floor. Breathe deeply.
3. Slowly release the posture and relax your head, back and elbows on the floor.

Benefits

1. It helps to cure lung diseases.
2. It regulates the function of thyroid glands.
3. It alleviates backache.

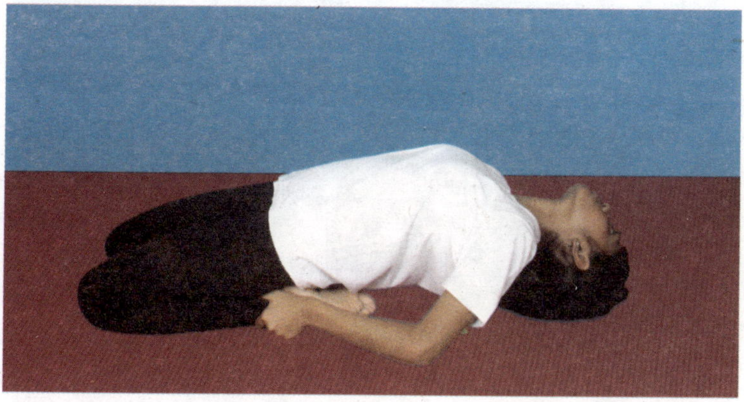

NAUKASANA
(Boat pose)

1. Lie flat on the floor keeping your arms straight besides your body.
2. Inhale and raise your head, arms and legs up from the floor.
3. Retain the breath and maintain this position as long as you can.
4. Slowly exhale, come down and relax.

Benefits

1. It helps in massaging the abdominal organs.
2. It tones all the organs.
3. It helps in removing lethargy.

BHUJANGASANA
(Cobra pose)

1. Lie on your stomach with your palms resting on the floor near your shoulders.
2. Let your chin touch the floor, feet together and your toes pointed outwards.
3. Inhale for two counts, raise your chin, head and chest above the ground and look up.
4. Retain your breath for the count of four.

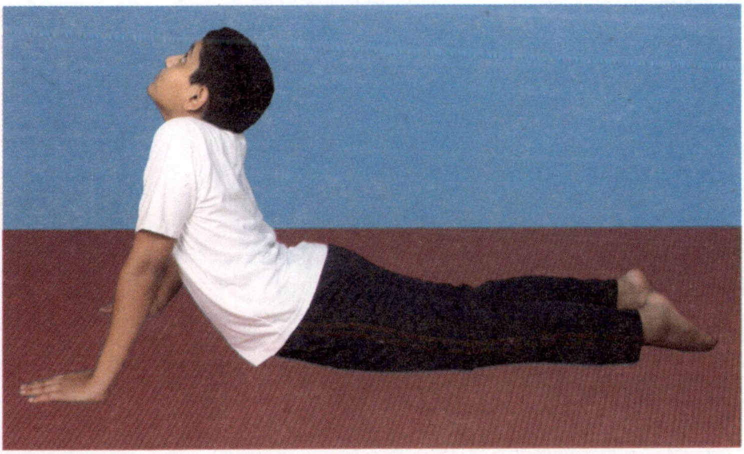

5. Exhale for two counts and slowly return to the ground.
6. Repeat three times.

Benefits

1. Strengthens the upper back muscles.
2. Builds up one's self esteem.

CHAKRASANA
(Wheel pose)

1. Lie down straight on your back.
2. Place your hands inverted, palms facing downward besides your shoulders.
3. Bend your knees and take your feet close towards the buttocks.
4. Breathe in, with the help of your hands raise your body and let your head down.
5. Hold the position till comfortable and slowly release yourself.

Benefits

1. Strengthens the arms and leg muscles.
2. Abdominal muscles are stretched.
3. Beneficial for migrane, asthma, back pain, stress and anxiety.

SALABHASANA
(Locust pose)

1. Lie down on the stomach with your hands below your thighs.
2. Inhale for two seconds and raise your right leg up. Keep in mind that your knee joint is straight.
3. Hold for four seconds.
4. Exhale for two seconds and slowly lower your leg down.
5. Repeat with the left leg.

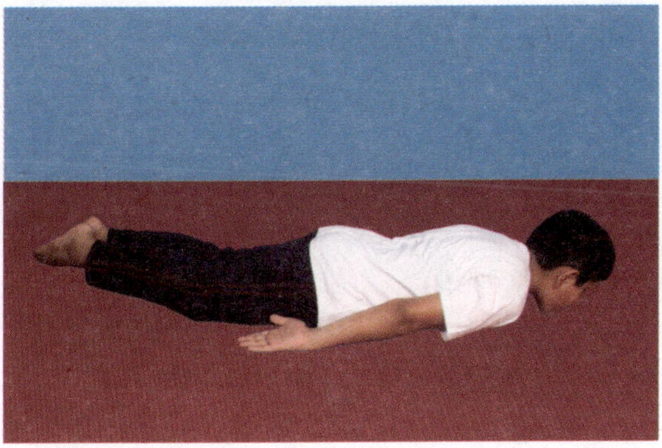

6. Complete three rounds on each side.
7. Then inhale, raise both your legs up straight for two seconds.
8. Retain for four seconds and remain in this position.
9. Exhale for two seconds and slowly lower your legs.

Benefits

1. It helps in relieving lower back pain.
2. It tones up the abdominal organs.

Dhanurasana
(Bow pose)

1. Lie down on the stomach with your legs together. Place your hands besides your body and chin touching the floor.
2. Bend your knees and hold your ankles.
3. Inhale for two seconds and raise your head, chest and thighs. Let your body rest on your abdomen.
4. Hold for four seconds.
5. Exhale for two seconds and slowly lower your body.
6. Repeat three times.

Benefits

1. It helps in relieving constipation and gas problem.
2. Relieves back pain and chest ailments.

Pranayama

Pranayama
(Equal breathing)

1. Sit in any meditative pose. Place your hands little above your knees on your thighs.
2. Gently close your eyes.
3. Slowly inhale for three seconds and exhale for three seconds.
4. Do five rounds of inhalation and five rounds of exhalation. Gradually increase these up to ten rounds.
5. Breathing should be slow, smooth and rhythmic.

Benefits

1. Controls anger and hyper-activeness.
2. It helps in keeping the mind calm.

Kapalbhati Pranayama
(Forceful exhalation)

1. Sit in any meditative posture.
2. Place your hands little above your knees on your thighs.
3. Breathe out forcibly for 15 counts.
4. Repeat for three times.

Benefit

It helps in increasing the lung capacity.

BHRAMARI PRANAYAMA
(Humming bee sound)

1. Sit in a comfortable meditative pose. Spine erect, head straight and the hands resting on the knees.
2. Close your eyes and relax for a minute.
3. The lips should remain gently closed with the teeth slightly separated throughout the practice. This allows the sound of vibration to be heard and felt more distinctly in the brain. Relax the jaws.
4. Raise the arms sideways and bend the elbows, bringing the hands to the ears. Use the index finger to plug the ears. The flaps of the ears may be pressed without inserting the fingers.
5. Bring the awareness to the centre of the head and keep the body absolutely still.
6. Breathe in through the nose.
7. Exhale slowly and in a controlled manner while making a deep, steady humming sound like that of a bee. Consider this as the first round this *asana*.

8. At the end of exhalation, breathe in deeply and repeat the process.
9. Perform five rounds.

Benefits

1. Relieves stress, mental tension, alleviates anger, insomnia and anxiety.
2. Reduces blood pressure.

Note: People suffering from ear infection should not practice this *asana*.

Concentration Kriyas

Trataka Kriya
(Eye exercise)

Guruji: Now, I will teach you an eye exercise, which will strengthen your eye muscles. If you do this regularly, you may never have to wear spectacles at all. *Trataka kriya* is the process of looking at a fixed point with fullest concentration, until tears come to one's eyes, so say the rishis.

Student: Is it the candle gazing exercise? I have heard about that.

Guruji: There are many techniques to do *trataka kriya* and every one of them has its merits.

1. Sit in Sukhasana or any other meditative pose, according to your convenience.
2. Stretch your left hand forward. Fix the eyes on your thumb.
3. Move your left hand towards the right shoulder continuously gazing at the thumb, keeping your head and neck straight. Similarly return the left hand to the starting position.
4. Repeat with the right hand.
5. Gently do palming.

Benefits

1. Strengthens the eye muscles.
2. Increases our concentration level.
3. Helps to get rid of laziness.

Candle Gazing

1. Sit in *sukhasana* for two minutes, with your eyes closed.
2. Place a lit candle in front of you at the eye level.
3. Slowly open your eyes and gaze at the wick of the candle.
4. After a minute, close your eyes and visualize the flame in front of your eyes.
5. Gently do the palming and open your eyes.

Benefit

Helps in achieving high concentration levels.

Relaxation Asanas

SAVASANA
(Corpse pose)

1. Lie down straight on the floor with your feet 12–18 inches apart, your arms about six inches apart, away from the body. Gently close your eyes.
2. Relax your body. Relax each and every part of your body one by one. Relax your toes, feet, soles, ankles, calves, knees, thighs, hips, abdomen, chest, shoulders, arms, palms, fingers, thumbs, lower back, upperback, neck, throat, chin, cheeks, nose, ears, eyes, forehead and head.
3. You will feel your body sinking to the floor.
4. When you feel relaxed, concentrate on your breathing.
5. Remain in this position for five minutes.
6. Gently move your fingers and toes. Open your eyes.
7. Inhaling stretch your arms upwards over your head and toes stretched outwards.

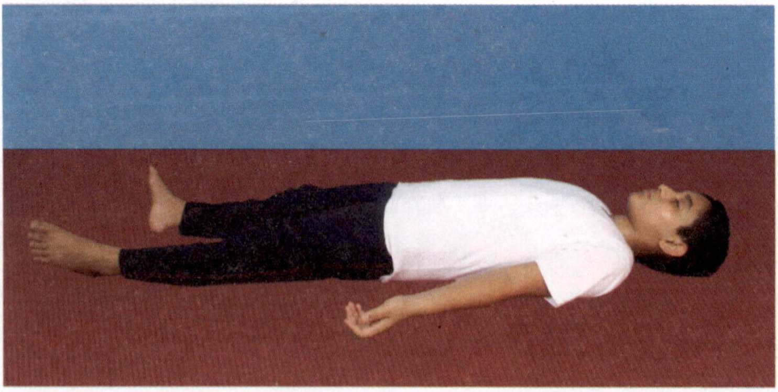

8. Turn to one side and with the support of your hands slowly sit up.

Benefits

1. This asana totally rejuvenates the body and mind.
2. We can rid our body from stiffness of the tissues and restlessness of mind.
3. Cures mood swings and cools ones temper.

Abdominal Breathing
(Diaphragmatic breathing)

1. Lie down on the floor. Bend your knees and keep your feet firm on the floor. Keep your knees together and feet close to your body.
2. Place your right hand on your abdomen and your left hand lying straight on the floor with your palms downwards.
3. Gently close your eyes.
4. While inhaling feel your abdomen rising up and while exhaling feel your abdomen moving downwards.
5. Relax in this position for five minutes.

Benefits

1. It creates an awareness of the breathing process.
2. It helps in reducing back pain.

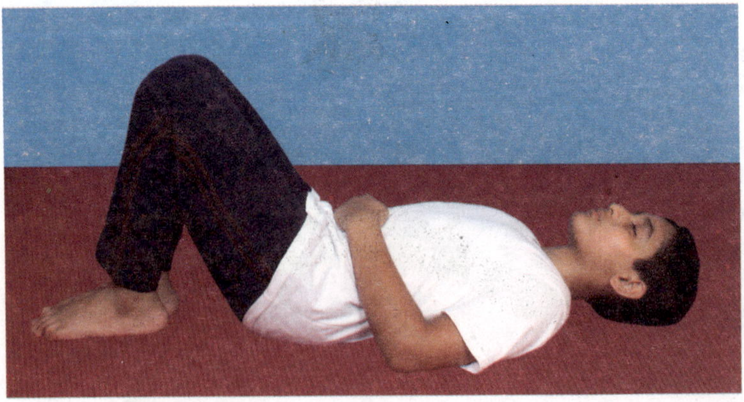

Nishp and Abhava
(No movement)

1. Sit on the floor and lean against the wall. Sit in a relaxed manner. Stretch your legs out with your feet 2–3 feet apart.
2. Place your hands on your thighs with palms facing upwards. Lean your head against the wall and gently close your eyes.
3. Listen to the sound of a vehicle passing by until you can hear it no more. Or the sound of a fan or any other fading sound, or the chirping of the birds till they fly away.
4. Relax in this position for 5–10 minutes.

Benefits

1. Helps in keeping a silent mind.
2. It relaxes our body.

Let's Talk about Food

By regular practice of yoga, one becomes the destroyer of all the problems. However, the most important thing is that only he who first pays attention to his diet can accomplish this. As per Yoga, food is not only for physical fitness but the right kind of food provides us with good mental health.

The food is divided into three categories based on the effects it has on our mind: *Satvik, Rajsik and Tamsik.*

Satvik food contains rich dietary fiber. It is rich in vitamins and minerals. It gives us energy. Vegetables, fruits, cereals, pulses, wheat, unpolished rice and milk fall under this category. Infact Yoga considers *Satvik* food to be the most superior type of food. It promotes longetivity, intelligence, health and happiness.

Rajsik food makes us more active, aggressive and excited. It causes indigestion and flatulence too. Spicy, oily, food, non-vegetarian food, tea, coffee, fermented products, polished rice is *Rajsik.*

Tamsik food makes us lazy, lethargic and dull. Stale food (more than 24 hours.), frozen food, preserved food (jam, cold drinks, biscuits, pickles), maida and its products, fall under this category.

A man selects food according to his taste and nature. Although human beings are considered the most intelligent of all the species, usually they do not eat, what is need or how much is needed. We all need food to live but we should take that food which gives us all the ingredients required by our body. We also need sufficient food in the right quantity and quality.

The essential nutrients needed by our body are, carbohydrates, proteins, fats, minerals and vitamins. These perform functions like growth, repair, energy and protection from diseases. However, there is no single item of food, which can provide us with all the necessary ingredients required for growth. It is therefore essential to eat a combination of foods, which provide us with all the necessary elements required by us. This is known as a *Balanced Diet.*

The quantity required of these vital elements is not the same for all of us. For example, an athelete would need a diet rich in carbohydrates to give him energy and a diet rich in proteins. Therefore, we must select our food according to our needs.

To keep our body healthy and fit, we must follow the principle of a balanced diet. I know you tend to get tempted by the attractively packaged food like chips, chocolates and aerated drinks. Avoiding them is difficult but we can definitely set limits.

Fruit juices, coconut water, lassi, milk shakes are an attractive alternative to aerated drinks. Likewise, for snacks—roasting, baking, grilling and boiling are equally tasty and healthy alternatives. The variety of vegetables, which blend with the potato to make a delicious cutlet or roll, is simply amazing.

One should always consume food in a clean and pleasant environment. It should be eaten slowly, and chewed well. Try to avoid watching television while eating as is commonly done, for the emotions felt while watching affects digestion of the food.

Conclusion

The chief objective of this book is to impress upon our dear reader the impressive and magical world of yoga.

I know the intellectual and inquisitive among you would always demand for a rational explanation of things put forth. Therefore, I have tried my best to convince you by explaining them in a scientific and rational manner.

In a nutshell, yoga will give you major benefits like better concentration, improved memory, freedom from stress and anxiety, increased peace and joy. You would develop better relations with friends, relatives, teachers and your family. You would notice a tremendous increase in self-confidence, self-esteem and self-reliance. You will learn to appreciate higher values, cultivate higher ideals, develop a deeper understanding of your culture and condition yourselves to a greater receptiveness in further learning. Well, all this besides the innumerable benefits of good health you receive as gifts.

Yoga practiced from an early age definitely leads to a healthier life style and steadiness in every aspect of one's life. It helps you in accepting any type of challenges in your lives and deal with them effectively.

The most important thing to remember in yoga is—success rests on regular practicing.

Here wishing you, happy exercising.

A healthier you,

And a happier you.

Synopsis

Attitude Training	... Yama and Niyama
Back Pain	... Bhujangasana, Dhanurasana and Salabhasana
Concentration	... Candle Gazing and Trataka
Co-ordination between Mind and Body	... Talasana and Utkat Asana
Digestion	... Vajrasana
Flexibility of the Spine	... Hastapadasana
Glow in the Face	... Simha Garjanasana
Headache	... Bhramari Pranayama and Kapalbhati Pranayama
Humility	... Yoga Mudra
Hyperactive	... Bhramari Pranayama, Equal Breathing and Mastsyasana
Meditative Asanas	... Padmasana and Vajrasana
Melodious Sound	... Simha Garjanasana
Reflection	... Vajrasana
Relaxation	... Abdominal Breathing, Makarasana, Nishp and Abhava, Pranayama and Savasana
Respiratory Problem	... Simha Garjanasana and Yoga Mudra
Self-Development	... Games play an important role
Spine Erect	... Padmasana and Parvatasana
Steadiness and One-Pointedness	... Ekapadasana and Sthitaprarthana Asana
Strengthening the Eyes	... Trataka
Tranquility of Mind	... Nishp and Abhava

Index